Ask Doctor Pete

Ask Doctor Pete

Dr Peter Rowan
Illustrated by Quentin Blake

to Betty
best wishes
Pete Rowan

JONATHAN CAPE
THIRTY-TWO BEDFORD SQUARE
LONDON

For my Mum and Dad

First published 1986
Text copyright © 1986 by Dr Peter Rowan
Illustrations copyright © 1986 by Quentin Blake
Jonathan Cape Ltd, 32 Bedford Square, London WC1B 3EL

British Library Cataloguing in Publication Data

Rowan, Peter
Ask Doctor Pete.
1. Health – Juvenile literature
I. Title   II. Blake, Quentin
613   RA777

ISBN 0-224-02869-3

Typeset by Computape (Pickering) Ltd, North Yorkshire
Printed in Great Britain by
The Alden Press, Oxford

Contents

Preface   7
"Does an apple a day keep the doctor away?"   9
"Why does my stomach rumble during school assembly?"   10
"When I was ill in bed Granny took all the flowers out of my room"   12
"Do the white bits in your nail show how much calcium you need?"   15
"Will eating fish make me brainy?"   16
"Is crying good for you?"   19
"My Mum says too many colds can make you deaf"   21
"My Mum makes me tuck my ears flat on the pillow at night"   22
"Can personal stereos make you deaf?"   23
"Some grown-ups say you should not sleep on your left side"   24
"My Mum says eating between meals will spoil my appetite"   25
"Can you make a baby stutter by tickling its feet?"   26
"My parents tell me to sit upright at the table or I will choke"   26
"Will chewing raw bacon give me worms?"   29
"My Dad says the best medicines taste the worst"   31
"Can you catch cold from sitting on wet grass?"   32
"Why do we put our tracksuits on after we've been running?"   33
"When I had injections the doctor seemed to stick the needle in anywhere"   35
"My teacher says not to sit on our school radiator as it causes piles"   37
"Can you get warts from touching toads?"   38
"My friend said if I picked dandelions I would wet the bed"   39
"Grown-ups say watching TV will damage your eyes"   41
"My Mum and Dad tell my younger brother not to play with his food"   43
"My Mum tells me not to run after drinking lemonade"   44
"Does thumb-sucking give you rabbit teeth?"   44
"Is it true that 'coughs and sneezes spread diseases'?"   45
"My Dad says you should rest after a big meal"   47
"My Grandad says he can blow smoke out of his ears"   49
"I get car-sick and my Dad says I should open one of the car windows"   50
"My Mum and Dad always make me wash my hands after going to the toilet"   51
"My dentist tells me not to eat sweets"   52
"Does eating bread crusts make your hair curl?"   53

"Does chocolate cause spots or migraine?" 54

"Is fresh air at the seaside good for you?" 55

"Does smoking stunt your growth?" 58

"If you sneeze with your eyes open will they pop out?" 59

"Does the Queen have blue blood?" 60

"Are brown eggs better for you than white eggs?" 61

"Do you get white fur on your tongue if you are constipated?" 63

"If I yawn my Mum tells me I am not getting enough sleep" 64

"My Mum can tell if I am tired by looking for bags under my eyes" 66

"After I have been outside my Mum tells me to take my coat off" 67

"My uncle says you can cure nettle stings by rubbing dock on your skin" 69

"There is a joke at school that eating baked beans makes you fart" 70

"Some people say you should put steak on a black eye" 72

"My parents say you should have a hot breakfast before going to school" 74

"I like cheesy things but grown-ups expect me to like sweet things" 75

"Why does our teacher tell us not to share combs, towels and shoes?" 77

"My Grandad says my nose bleeds because I pick it." 78

"My Grandad says he used to brush his hair a hundred times a day" 81

"If you frown and the wind changes will your face stay that way?" 81

"Do carrots make you see in the dark?" 82

"When there was an eclipse of the sun we looked at it with dark glasses" 83

"My Granny says green apples will make me run to the toilet" 85

"I have trouble getting to sleep when I stay at my friend's house" 86

"My Mum tells me to run the tap in the morning before having a drink" 87

"Is it true you shouldn't drink from the hot tap?" 89

"Why does Granny give me onions when I have a cold?" 89

"Should you feed a cold and starve a fever?" 91

"A boy at school says talking to yourself is the first sign of madness" 92

"Do poisonous mushrooms only grow under trees?" 94

"My brother says bang your head on the pillow to make sure you wake up" 96

Preface

It seems strange to think back over the fear I had during my first stay in hospital at the age of seven. Would I pull through after refusing to eat the boiled fish? Well I managed to. Not only that, I survived other dangers grown-ups warned me about, like not wearing a vest in winter and sitting on the school radiators. It seems funny now, but it wasn't at all at the time.

Of course the real problem was to decide what was true and what was not. Sometimes people believed sincerely what they told you but they could not explain why. They had heard it from their parents, or it was an "old wives' tale" from way back in folklore. Sometimes people were just having you on. And who is going to worry about eating berries in the woods if the person who told you not to also says that touching dandelions will make you wet the bed?

I wish I could have had this book then. I think it would have made life seem a little more straightforward, and would have got rid of many doubts.

1986   DOCTOR PETE

"Does an apple a day keep the doctor away?"

Crunching an apple won't mend a broken leg or cure a bout of the measles, of course; but apples *are* good for you and help to keep you healthy, for a number of reasons.

First they are a natural food which contain a large amount of what is called fibre or roughage. Lots of food fads that suddenly interest adults (and some doctors) are little more than just that – fashions. However, the recent trend in the Western world towards a high fibre diet is a good one. Many of the under-developed countries already have diets full of fibre, and they have largely

avoided some illnesses which are quite common in the West.

One of the main benefits of a high fibre diet is that the bowels work much better on bulky food which has not had all the natural roughage taken out. In the past, when the expression "An apple a day" was first used, people realised that fruit like the apple helped to prevent constipation, although they didn't have all the scientific knowledge we have now. Instead of believing it to be the effect of the fibre, they thought raw apple juice helped the breakdown of food in the intestine.

Another reason apples are good for you lies in their crunchiness. When you bite into one it tends to clean your teeth. You still have to brush your teeth, though. Bits of apple that lodge between the teeth have sugars in them which can cause damage to the enamel if they are given the time. So not only will an apple help to keep the doctor away, it might even have a similar effect on the dentist's drill.

"Why does my stomach rumble during school assembly?"

Your stomach usually rumbles when you are hungry. Just the thought of food will set it churning, rather like an empty cement mixer. This is what is called a reflex action. A famous Russian called Pavlov was the first to notice it. He had some dogs in his laboratory which were usually fed at midday. Some bells nearby happened to be rung at the same time. After a while Pavlov noted that the dogs' mouths watered at noon when the bells rang whether there was food about or not. He called this a conditioned reflex because the link between bells and food had been conditioned in the dogs' minds.

Going back to the noisy stomach at school: you hear it rumble in assembly probably because it is quiet and possibly also because you are slightly nervous. The thought of lessons, or even of other people hearing your tummy rumble, could be making you swallow air. You will have seen other quite normal people gulp nervously. If air gets into your tummy like this and the stomach then moves as it is always doing, you will hear the rumble in the quiet assembly hall.

A similar thing can happen at the dinner table. During a gap in the conversation you can often hear people's stomachs churning up the meal they have just eaten and starting to squirt it into the next part of the gut. It tends to be less of a deep rumble, though, because the stomach is full. Some people find this embarrassing but it's perfectly natural and, in any case, there's nothing you can do about it. The body can make all sorts of noises. Some – like a heart beat – you need a stethoscope to hear.

You can in fact make a stethoscope of sorts yourself. In 1816 a man called Laënnec made the first one using a rolled up piece of paper and putting his ear at one end and the other end on someone's chest. Later on he used a wooden tube. Nowadays doctors tend to use flexible rubber tubes but you can hear the heartbeat in a quiet room using the cardboard centre of a toilet roll, just as Laënnec did with his roll of paper.

The old-fashioned type of stethoscope is still used for listening to the hearts of unborn babies.

The stethoscope is also useful for listening to the lungs for abnormal breath sounds like wheezes; and you can listen over narrowed arteries in places like the neck. You can sometimes hear a noise just like river water rushing under a bridge. When this happens the doctor knows something is wrong because a normal wide blood vessel does not make a noise; just as you do not hear a river unless it is forced to gush through a narrow channel.

Body noises can be loud enough to be heard without a stethoscope. They are usually noises from somewhere in the belly, and they often amuse or embarrass people. A few find them useful. There was a Frenchman years ago who made quite a good living in music halls by "letting off" to a number of popular tunes.

"When I was ill in bed Granny looked after me. She used to be a nursing sister in a big hospital and every night she took all the flowers out of my bedroom."

She meant well. Some years ago it was the custom to take flowers out of hospital wards every night. The reason for this goes back hundreds of years. It is all to do with flowers using up oxygen in the air.

Oxygen is a vital part of air. We need to breathe it in to stay alive. Our bodies burn it up with food, in the same way that cars use it with petrol. Coal fires also need it to keep going.

Indirectly this shows how a fire could kill you. If you were trapped by one, you might suffocate because the fire had used all the oxygen in the air. And if you run a car engine in an enclosed space like a garage, you can fall unconscious and die. The car engine converts oxygen into the poisonous gas, carbon monoxide.

It was only two hundred or so years ago that scientists worked out the importance of oxygen to the body. It was known that if you put an animal in a closed container it would suffocate and die. But it was not until 1774 that an Englishman called Joseph Priestley discovered this colourless gas oxygen, which makes up 20 per cent of air.

It was realised then that all animals need oxygen to survive. They take it into the lungs when they breathe in and give out carbon dioxide when they breathe out. This is the gas which would suffocate you if you were stupid enough to put your head in a plastic bag.

After he found out about animals and oxygen Priestley discovered that green plants seem to do the opposite.

That is, they take in carbon dioxide out of the air and give out oxygen. Naturally enough the result was an amazing boom in the use of plants in sick-rooms. Bedrooms and hospital wards were turned into virtual greenhouses.

Later a Dutch doctor called Ingen-Housz worked out what really happens when plants "breathe".

Green plants can only take in carbon dioxide and give out oxygen in very bright light. They do this to make stores of sugar. When it gets dark the plants need oxygen to turn their sugar into energy. During this process they take oxygen from the air and release carbon dioxide back into it. Thus *at night* the plants "breathe" like we do.

Once people knew this it became the custom, until only a few years ago, to take plants and flowers out of patients' rooms at night in case the carbon dioxide collected and harmed the sick.

Nowadays this is known to be a waste of nursing time as the amounts of gases involved are so small.

However, anyone who still does this is trying to do the best for the invalid he or she is looking after. And also it is an opportunity to remove any dead flowers and put fresh water into the vase.

"My friend's Mum says the white bits in your fingernail show how much calcium you need. Is this true?"

No, I'm afraid she's got it wrong. Calcium is an important element that occurs in the body in lots of forms. And it does lots of things. But you can't tell how much you need by looking at the white bits in your nails.

Perhaps this belief came about because limestone, which is a form of calcium, is white. (It's better known as chalk.) Or because bones look white not just outside the body, but also in X-rays. Or because white milk is a rich source of calcium.

The white flecks in your nails are caused by banging them and causing damage. What you can see of the nail is dead tissue, like hair (which is why you can cut your nails without it hurting). But at the base under the skin is the nail bed from which the nail forms and grows out. When this is knocked it produces a white fleck in the nail that is being formed at that particular moment.

The knock needs only be so very slight that you can't even remember it as you see the white fleck grow over the next six months. That means if you bang your nail at Christmas the mark it leaves will be clipped off the end of the fingernail during the next year's summer holidays.

These white flecks are nothing to do with the white half-moons which most people have at the nail base. They appear white because at that particular place the nail is not attached very firmly to the flesh underneath. Where the nail appears pink it is held on well, and you are seeing the red blood in your finger shining through the nail.

Some people do not have half-moons at all. This is not

abnormal, but it does make them an unreliable guide for the doctor, who looks at them for signs of illness. Half-moons do change in some conditions, though. If you get very anaemic and short of red blood cells then they seem to disappear because the whole nail looks pale.

Nails can still be a good guide to the doctor. Signs of many illnesses show up in them. One common skin problem called psoriasis causes tiny pits to form in nails. Any bad infection that lays you up in bed will slow growth down for a while. This shows itself as a ridge in the nail. You will not see it at the time; only later as it grows out. So as a gypsy looks at your palm to read your future, the doctor can often look at your nails and see what you have been up to in the past.

"My aunt says I should eat a lot of fish as it will make me brainy."

Nonsense. Eat a lot of fish by all means as it's a very good source of protein, but don't expect it to make you clever. Some people claim that celery will make you brainy, but there's no truth in that either.

The reasons behind all these odd beliefs about food that grown-ups have are interesting. Many are repeated because your parents heard them from their parents; perhaps in this case as a way of trying to get someone who didn't like fish to eat it.

Some doctors have reported that very severe starvation of protein can lead to a child's brain suffering. This could be misread by an anxious adult to mean fish (high in protein) is necessary to make a child clever.

Maybe it was because white fish does, with some imagination, look a little like brain tissue. Or because of certain fats called lecithins, which are found in fish and are vital to the nervous system. But it is not necessary for you to eat fish to get them. In fact the word lecithin comes from the Greek word "lekithos" meaning yolk.

So there's no truth in the saying that eating fish will make you brainy. Working hard at school is the best way.

Having said that, it is important to put in a good word for fish as a food and to explain why boiled white fish is often given to sick people.

When you are growing you need a lot of protein. Protein is made of what are called amino acids. There are some twenty-two of these in our bodies and they are like the building blocks that make up a house.

When you are ill as a child, your growth tends to slow down, so as you recover it is even more important to eat foods with protein in order to catch up.

White fish is almost all protein. It has hardly any fat. (Oily fish like herring, mackerel, tuna, sardines and salmon have more.)

The fact that it has very little fat makes it quick and easy for the body to digest, as fatty meals delay the stomach emptying. When you have been ill, perhaps even been sick, that is the last thing you need.

This is why some people say pork is an indigestible meat. Certain cuts have a high fat content and so make you feel full very easily.

Boiled fish is therefore a very sensible food to give someone recovering after an illness.

I remember having boiled fish at the age of seven when I was in hospital and the sight and smell of it made me feel ill again.

These days, though, there are much more tasty ways to serve it up so that this doesn't happen. And I bet your Mum knows better ways to cook it. Like poaching or steaming. Not only will the fish taste nice, but cooking it lightly avoids the risk of boiling much of the goodness out.

"Is crying good for you?"

It can be. There are all sorts of reasons why humans cry. If you cry for a good reason (like toothache) and the problem then gets some treatment, then that is clearly a good thing. (And if you think about it, a cry is the only way a very young baby can tell its mother there's a nappy pin sticking in its bottom.)

If it simply prevents you from bottling up your feelings then it is also good. It may make your parents realise how you feel. It is not always easy for children or adults to put feelings into words. In many ways, then, a good cry can relieve tension, like a good laugh.

You may have noticed that young babies cry a lot. In fact when they are born they often cry straightaway and this is a very good way of filling the lungs with air.

As the baby progresses through its first year it cries less. So at six months it will put up with a wetter nappy than at one month. However, the number of things which make it cry increases. Things like being cold or hungry. It's very difficult to be absolutely certain about these sorts of things in babies because they can't actually tell you what is wrong.

It is interesting that animals do not cry because they are sorry about something, although marine turtles will cry when they are laying eggs.

This is because, living in the sea, they have to get rid of a certain amount of salt to keep the balance right between their body's salt and that of the sea. Excess salt goes out in their tears. Whether the strain of laying lots of eggs has anything to do with bringing tears to their eyes, no one knows. As with young babies, you don't really know what's going through their minds.

Incidentally, crocodiles also shed similar tears. No one knows why. Most crocodiles live in fresh water so the situation is not the same as for marine turtles.

As most people know, crocodiles will eat you given half a chance. Apparently they have been seen to cry after doing this and that's where the expression "shedding crocodile tears" comes from. These are "false" tears that mean you are not at all sorry for what you have just done.

To finish with another saying that links animals and crying. This one is different and important to understand. "Crying wolf" can be a dangerous thing to do. If you cry for attention too often when there is nothing wrong, then you may be ignored when you really need help. This is an example of when crying is not good for you.

"My Mum says too many colds can make you deaf."

S he is right. Out of every 1,000 children in the country at the moment about twenty are partially deaf. The cause of this deafness is usually an ear infection which hasn't cleared up. Sticky mucus can collect behind the ear-drum and gum it up. In fact it's actually called glue ear. Imagine trying to play a drum that's been filled with treacle! That is one reason why parents worry about ear infections and are so fussy about them.

Teachers get involved because it is at school that the problem really shows itself. If you can't hear what the teacher says, you will find it harder to understand and learn things.

"My Mum makes me tuck my ears flat on the pillow at night because she says they will start to stick out. Is doing this worth it?"

No. If you are going to have ears that stick out, "bat ears", this is going to happen anyway. And turning the question around the other way – if your ears stick out, taping them flat on your head is also a waste of time.

Quite a lot of people have ears that stick out. If it becomes a real worry then there is a simple operation which will put things right. The doctor won't do this until you're about five because the ears haven't finished growing until then.

"I have been told that listening to personal stereos can make you deaf. Can it?"

Yes it can. Any loud noise can make children deaf and adults too.

It is best not to have the volume up high even for a little while. These stereos are a great idea if they are used properly. The problems start when you try to do something like cycling with them on. It seems too obvious to say but quite a few daft people have had accidents on the road because they couldn't hear things like a car hooter. And if you're listening to your favourite record, how can you concentrate on the traffic?

Noise is measured in decibels (dB).

A ticking watch is under 20 dB. Talking is about 60. Loud music is 80. Pneumatic drills and jet aircraft are well over 120.

Anything over 80 dB can damage your hearing so badly you can't get it back. The message is clear. Be careful with the volume.

"I have heard grown-ups say that you should not sleep on your left side."

Yes, I've heard this. It's a load of rubbish. The reason people believe it is because the heart is on the left side. They think your body weight is in some way causing it harm. Another similar saying which is more difficult to understand is that you should not sleep with your arms above your head. The reason usually given is that this somehow affects the circulation of blood through the heart. They are all wrong. Sleep how you like. Apart from anything else everyone moves around during a night's sleep. So however you start off you are unlikely to be in that position for long. Can you imagine how many damaged hearts there would be if this old tale were true!

One last thought on hearts. In a very few people the heart is actually on the right side of the body.

In the James Bond story *Dr No* the villain is tortured and finally the gang decide to finish him off by shooting him through the heart. He survives because he is "one in a million" with his heart on the other side of the body.

"My Mum says that eating between meals will spoil my appetite."

Of course it will. If you fill up at 11 in the morning your stomach is hardly going to be empty at midday for another meal. The trouble with "between meals food" is that it often tends to be poor in things like protein which you must have for growth. It may just be poor quality, full stop. Crisps and sweets may taste good and may give you energy, but they don't give you what your body needs for things like building muscle. So it does you no good at all to spoil your appetite for a good, well-balanced meal by eating foods that fill but do not nourish you.

"Can you make a baby stutter by tickling its feet?"

No. It's important to realise that normal young children up to the age of about four or five can seem to stutter as they hurry to get words out. This actually disappears as the words become more familiar and easy to use. However, occasionally the problem causes so much worry to the child that a real stutter then develops.

"My parents tell me to sit upright at the table or I will choke."

You can swallow food standing on your head if you want to. The muscular gullet will force food towards the stomach. You often see adults slumped in armchairs eating food virtually lying down.

And if you think about it, a lot of animals have to rely on this muscle power to swallow. When a horse puts its head down to drink from a trough, the water actually travels uphill on the way "down" to the stomach.

So you will not choke. Gravity is not necessary.

However, that does not mean you should not sit upright at the table if your parents tell you to. One good reason is that if you get into a bad habit of slumping forward it could eventually leave you with round shoulders. Another reason is plain good manners. Just think how awful you look to the people around you if you are slumped over the table.

Whatever position you are in, though, it is worth chewing your food properly and eating it slowly. Digestion starts well before you put food in your mouth and swallow it. Just seeing and smelling food automatically activates the saliva. Food needs to be well chewed and mixed with this. The saliva contains digestive juices which start to break down the food so that the body can make use of it. The agents of this breakdown are the enzymes. They are the chemical compounds in the

digestive juices which act just like the enzymes in biological washing powder. Instead of breaking down dirt they break down food.

When the mixture of food and saliva reaches the stomach more juices are added. The stomach adds strong acid as well and churns it all up like a washing machine.

If you swallow large pieces of food without chewing them the stomach has to work a lot harder. Also, eating quickly can mean you swallow too much air. This can be uncomfortable and make you burp. If you really irritate your stomach by the way you load your food in, it will simply throw it all back at you.

Dogs can bolt their food. (In the wild the fastest eater will get the most food.) They can get away with this because, for their size, they have much bigger stomachs than we have.

If you are about to be sick, you may notice that you suddenly salivate more. This could be to protect the mouth and teeth from the acid in the stomach that may be on its way up. This hydrochloric acid is very strong. If, for example, you are sick into a cotton handkerchief and the vomit is not washed off, the stomach acids can burn a hole in it. It's amazing really that the stomach does not dissolve itself. Sometimes its protective slimy coating does break down. Then the acid burns a hole in the stomach wall. If the acid runs up into the gullet where there is no protection it will burn there too. This is commonly called heartburn.

'I like chewing raw bacon but my Mum says it could give me worms.'

There is a risk of getting tapeworms if you eat raw or undercooked pork. It can happen with beef too and also with fish in certain parts of the world.

This is uncommon in countries where farmers "worm" their pigs and cows, and where there are strict rules for handling meat and inspectors watch carefully for signs of worms in meat.

However, it is still not wise to eat raw beef or pork. The heat of cooking will kill any tapeworms that may have slipped through.

These tapeworms are only one variety of the many such parasites that can infect humans.

They come in various shapes and sizes, often have quite complicated lives and may live in the guts or in other parts of the body. They may even spend part of their life-cycle in other animals.

The tapeworm we have just spoken about can be yards long and lives part of its life in pigs, cattle or fish.

An adult "fish" tapeworm can grow to 14 metres! It seems incredible that one of these could live inside you. Especially as the total length of a man's guts is only about 9 metres. I've never seen one this long, but I'm told that they have to curl up to fit in.

They can cause some strange problems. The worm is very partial to a vitamin called B_{12}. Shortage of this can then lead to an unusual form of anaemia.

Threadworms are another sort and much commoner. They look just like white threads of cotton, ½ to 1 cm long. You may not know you have them until you see them after using the toilet. Sometimes they can make your bottom itch. This is because the female worm

comes out from inside you at night to lay her eggs on your skin! This is what irritates and itches.

Hookworm is another one of these pests. It is only common in warm countries and lives happily in the part of the guts called the duodenum. This is the tube-like part after the stomach. These worms are about 1 cm long and hook into the lining wall of the duodenum. This can cause some slight blood loss. If it goes on for a long time, the patient may become short of blood from sheltering these unwelcome guests. In fact hookworm is a common cause of anaemia in the world. Not surprising as over 400 million people have them!

It is important to realise that many of these worms cause no serious problems at all. Also they are usually easily treated, and anyone can catch them. Like having nits, there is nothing to be ashamed of.

Grown-ups often say if you eat a lot you "must have worms". This is hardly ever true. However, they probably get the idea from the fact that a few patients with tapeworms do lose weight and feel very hungry.

One final word of warning though. The common childhood worms like threadworms are passed on mainly by people who do not wash their hands after going to the toilet.

"My Dad says the best medicines taste the worst."

That's not really true any more. These days a lot of care goes into making medicines taste nice. Given a choice, doctors will choose the medicines that children will like and therefore take. So drugs companies stand to make a lot of money, if they come up with a popular brand.

When your Dad was young, this was less likely to be true and a lot of good medicines did taste awful. People told their children that it was the best to encourage them to take it. Two very popular medicines were aspirin and paracetamol. In their basic form most children found them bitter and unpleasant.

A lot of medicines that you may need can be taken in various ways. So if you do not like taking tablets, even crushed up in your food, ask if the same thing comes as a liquid.

"Can you catch a cold from sitting on wet grass or going out with wet hair?"

No. Colds are infections caused by germs called viruses. They are not caused by cold weather, damp ground or going out with wet hair.

This idea probably arose because there are more colds about in winter. The reason for this is partly that these particular viruses tend to strike during this season; just as there are other kinds that are more common in summer. (They tend to cause tummy upsets.) Also, it is easier for colds to spread from person to person in the winter. When it's cold places like schools and offices tend to have

the windows shut. Heating systems may circulate the air and help to spread the colds. That's one reason why it is often thought to be healthy to open windows for fresh air.

There is a place in Salisbury, Wiltshire, called the Common Cold Unit. They have carried out tests on all this. People have been sat in draughts and had buckets of cold water tipped over them to see what happens. They may be cold and wet, but they do not catch colds. It's strange to think that some people are prepared to go and spend spare time being treated like this and being sprayed with germs.

One thing cold air can trigger, particularly if it is dry, is an asthma attack. This fact may explain the notion that you should wear a vest in winter to avoid getting "chesty" or a scarf across your face if it is very cold.

Asthma comes from a Greek word meaning "panting". Lots of causes can set off a bout of wheezing, a common one being breathing in some sort of dust. However, simply breathing in cold air can do it. This could make you "chesty" on a cold day if you have the tendency.

"After we've been running in athletic races at school we are told to put our tracksuits on. Why?"

The sensible reason for this is that without some extra clothing over your vest and running shorts you will soon get cold.

When you run, your body burns up energy. This produces a lot of heat just like a coal fire. The body has to get rid of this heat to keep its temperature normal.

One way is by sweating. As the sweat evaporates into the air it cools you.

With little clothing on this happens very quickly. Exactly the same thing can happen if you swim and dry off in the wind. That is why your parents may ask you to dry off with a towel after you have been for a swim in the sea.

If the body loses too much through this evaporation of water or sweat from the skin, it has to make its own heat to keep itself warm. One way it does it automatically is by shivering. Shivering is just muscle movement producing heat. The same effect is gained by using muscles in running around to "get warm".

However, when you shiver all the muscles are used. Even the ones around your mouth. That's why your teeth chatter when you shiver. The muscles are working to make heat and knocking them together like a pair of castanets.

When you are running a race you need to lose heat, otherwise you could overheat like a car with no water in its radiator.

Once you have stopped, though, you need some kind of covering like a tracksuit so that your body doesn't lose too much heat. It's like putting a blanket over the engine of a car in winter.

"When I have had injections, the doctor seemed to stick the needle in anywhere. My Dad says he had loads when he was in the Army and they always went for the left arm."

To deal with your Dad's left arm first. Some medical people used to favour a particular arm. There were a variety of reasons for this; as usual a few made sense and a few did not. One which didn't was that the left arm is closer to the heart than the right arm. This is true; but it does not affect the injection one little bit. The drug is not going to act better or faster or be any more likely to damage the heart.

Another reason why the left arm was chosen does make some sense. The injections which your Dad is likely to have had often made the arm very sore. If you were right-handed (as nine out of ten people are), it was better to have your left arm stiff and unusable. The Army was very thoughtful in these matters! I suppose it was bad luck if you were left-handed!

The reason why injections made the arm sore (unlike the injections you had about the time you started school) was because they would have been for different diseases altogether. Some of the vaccines you needed to go abroad made the arm really tender. This is why a lot of ex-servicemen can remember their injections so well. You need not worry about this. Some of these vaccines – like the one against smallpox – are not even necessary now as the disease has been wiped out.

Now back to your injections. It may seem that doctors and nurses stick them in anywhere; but I can assure you they don't. A lot of thought goes into choosing a place. For an injection into a muscle the ideal area is large, easy to inject and, most important, free of things that the

needle could damage like nerves or arteries. It is not surprising, then, why the muscular backside is often chosen. Some doctors use the arm. Some the muscles of the thigh.

But a lot think that the backside is supreme. All you have to do is divide one cheek up into imaginary quarters, then stick your needle into the upper outer quarter. This almost certainly guarantees you will only hit muscle. And, most important, you'll miss the sciatic nerve. This is the biggest nerve in the body and runs down to the leg under the big gluteus maximus muscle. (That's the one you sit on.)

Quite a few of you will become doctors or nurses one day. This is a very useful tip you might remember.

A word about people who tell you you are not going to feel an injection. I can remember being told this by a dentist when I was a boy. It only took a few visits before I realised that either he had never had a needle stuck in him or he was a liar.

Of course you feel them. What is true, though, is that they're not going to hurt. This is usually correct.

In the mid 1960s there was a move in the United Kingdom towards disposable needles for injections. A needle was only used once then thrown away.

Before this time doctors and nurses had to boil up needles (and a lot of other pieces of equipment) and re-use them. I do not remember this myself but nurses who are older than I am can remember needles getting blunter and blunter until they were really difficult to stick through the skin. These injections probably were more painful. (Your Dad would have had to put up with this sort of thing.)

A final word about pain. A very important thing is how you think about it. A kick on the shin when you are scoring the winning goal is felt far less than if you were expecting the same kick from the school bully. In fact you may not even notice it at the time on the soccer pitch. This is because the brain can handle pain in different ways, and make you feel differently about it.

That's why doctors and nurses make light of the whole business of having an injection. Clearly, though, it's important not to pretend that you are not going to feel it. That can only work once.

Do not be frightened of injections. They are given for good reasons. And in the end you will probably avoid a lot more pain by having them.

"My teacher says not to sit on our school radiator; she says it causes piles."

My teacher used to say this. They must learn it at teacher training college. It's not true.

Piles are swollen blood vessels. They are a bit like the varicose veins you can get in the legs except that these occur in your bottom. Sometimes they pop out into the outside world, and look like a bunch of purple grapes. They are quite common in adults. The best way of avoiding them is to eat a high fibre diet so that going to the toilet is easy and painless. Straining is one cause of them. Heat is not.

"Can you get warts from touching toads?"

No. The poor old toad is much maligned about this. Perhaps because it has a "warty" skin itself. However, these are not true warts like the ones caused by viruses.

In fact the toad itself is sometimes used to "charm" warts away.

There isn't a *brilliant* way of getting rid of warts; and they will probably go on their own anyway.

The ways that doctors use are not a lot more successful than the old-fashioned ways that sometimes enlisted the help of a toad.

Some country areas still have professional wart charmers who do things like rub meat on a wart and then feed the meat to the dog. The idea is that the unlucky dog gets the wart instead. Other traditional cures involve doing other spooky and rather mysterious things. Cotton is tied around the wart. Slug or snail slime is applied. The wart charmer may advise that the sufferer stands outside at midnight holding a frog. Much of the value of this is in convincing the wart sufferer that what he or she is doing will be effective.

There is no doubt that this sort of suggestion works. Doctors showed in one experiment, which was published in the highly respectable medical journal *The Lancet*, that warts can be hypnotised away. And hypnotism is only a form of suggestion.

Many medicines seem to gain much of their power through this sort of faith.

"My friend said that if I picked dandelions and got the milk in the stems on my hands, I would wet the bed."

I can remember it worrying me a lot. It's *not* true. But like a lot of these sayings there is something behind it all.

The dandelion has in it a drug called a diuretic. This makes you pass extra water. A similar thing happens to the body whenever you drink a lot. Perhaps extra orange juice at a party.

A lot of older people take diuretics for conditions like blood pressure. Take a diuretic pill in the morning and you are quite likely to have to make extra trips to the toilet until midday. (This is why patients take them in the morning. You could take them at night, but only if you were keen to keep getting out of bed.)

Diuretics have various effects within the kidneys. The main one is that as the kidneys filter the blood to make the urine, the diuretics allow extra fluid to pass out of the blood along with the waste products.

There are a lot of very good diuretics now that are manufactured from chemicals. But in the old days a build-up of water in the body had to be treated by natural drugs such as that contained in the dandelion leaf. The conditions which were being treated then were much the same as today. When fluid builds up in the body it often collects around the ankles. This used to be called dropsy. As soon as it was noted, out came the dandelion leaf. And the patient had to run to pass the water when the drug started to work. If you were in bed when it worked ... well, you can see how the story about touching dandelions and bedwetting must have begun.

The French must have an idea about all this. Their

name for dandelion is "pissenlit". "En lit" means "in bed".

Wetting the bed is quite common in young children and hardly ever means that anything's wrong. In fact one child in ten starting school wets the bed. Not many people know about it because it's not something you boast about in the playground, so if you are in this group you are not alone. As a matter of interest three years of age seems to be the commonest age to become dry at night.

If you get as far as seeing the doctor about the habit, he may ask about "worms" because threadworms can irritate you during the night and having unsettled the sleep, result in a wet bed. This is rare. Generally there is no serious physical cause to worry about.

Eventually nearly everyone stops; and that's usually when grown-ups stop making it into a big thing.

No one fully understands why some children are slow to learn control of the bladder at night. Most doctors, though, believe being anxious about it (and other things) only further postpones the day (or rather night) when wet beds are no more.

"I have heard grown-ups say that watching a lot of TV will damage your eyes."

This is just not true. If it were there would be a lot of adults who would damage their eyes before any of the children.

Like doing anything to excess, though, watching a lot of TV isn't a very good idea. In America it has been worked out now that by the age of three American children may spend 25–30 hours watching TV every week. While this may not cause any physical harm (except perhaps a sore behind from sitting) it is obviously a lot of time to fritter away. And, more important, if the programmes are rubbish then the young child may start to think along the same lines and not realise there is anything better.

Even the good programmes cannot compare to the excitement of real life or a well-written adventure story. If you are spending seven hours a day in front of the telly you are clearly missing out on other things.

Another question is whether reading in poor light damages your eyes. As someone who first read all the James Bond books by the light of a torch under the bedclothes at my boarding school I have always had an interest in this.

The answer is that it does not damage the eyes. It may make them ache, though. When you read in poor light you tend to hold the book close. This is especially true when you are under the bedclothes with a torch!

Now when you look at a book close-up the eye has to do two important things: first it has to focus. It does not do this like a camera. Muscles actually change the shape of the lens. For near work these ciliary muscles contract. Ligaments holding the eye are relaxed. And the lens, which has an elastic cover, gets fatter.

Second, as you have two eyes, muscles outside the eye have to line them up so that they both look at the same part of your book. (If they did not you would notice double vision.)

So here are two sets of muscles working hard, perhaps in the glare of torchlight. It is not surprising that you may notice your eyes aching. And while no permanent damage is being done, any weakness that the eye already has may show up, perhaps as a squint.

All in all it's best to read in good light with the book at a comfortable distance.

Ideally as you read this, the book should be about 45 centimetres away.

"My Mum and Dad are always telling my younger brother not to play with his food. What's wrong in making castles out of his mashed potato? He always eats it afterwards."

Very young children can't tell playtime from meal-time. You just have to let them get on and make a mess.

When you get older you have to fit in with the rest of the family. Sitting around together to eat is an important gathering in all families in countries all over the world. Other people may not want to wait while you play.

Also, if you make a mess someone has to clear it up and it's better to learn to eat properly at home than learning the hard way at school. Would you want to be hit by flying porridge? It's best to keep eating and playing separate. Besides, the food gets cold while you play with it and may not taste as good when you do get round to eating it.

"My Mum tells me not to run after drinking lemonade."

It's best not to. The fizziness in the lemonade will blow up your stomach, as if it were a football. Try shaking the lemonade before you drink it and see what happens!

Apart from feeling uncomfortable, a bloated stomach can give you hiccups. It presses up on the muscle under the lungs and irritates it. When this muscle starts to twitch in annoyance air in the lungs is sucked in past your vocal cords. The noise that results is called a hiccup. Your body is trying to get rid of the excess gases that shaking up the lemonade has released from the stomach. The next stage if it tries harder is actually to make you be sick.

Eating food quickly can do the same thing as the lemonade.

"Does thumb-sucking give you rabbit teeth?"

Rabbits have front teeth that stick out slightly. If you suck your thumb a lot over a long period of time, that is, for months, the continued pulling forward as you suck on the thumb can make your teeth stick out. (It's the same way that braces change the position of teeth.)

It doesn't matter before the age of six because the second set of permanent teeth have not appeared. If your milk teeth turn out to be like a rabbit's it's less important

as they are going to drop out and be replaced. After six it's best not to do a lot of thumb-sucking, although it's a fairly harmless pastime apart from this effect on the teeth. It certainly will not stunt your growth as some people seem to think.

"Is it true that 'coughs and sneezes spread diseases'?"

Yes. When you sneeze air is shot out at about 160 km per hr. That's the speed of a hurricane. A cough clocks in a bit slower at about 100 km per hr. But that's still faster than the speed most cars travel at. And the droplets have germs in them. If you sneeze because

you have a cold the germs can infect the person you sneeze over. The same thing can happen with a cough. Both sneezing and coughing are the result of irritation. In the case of sneezing the lining of the nose has been irritated. With coughing it is the lungs.

It is very unkind, rude and inconsiderate to cough and sneeze over people. The best place to sneeze is in your handkerchief.

If you have ever played "Ring a Ring of Roses" you will remember the line "Atishoo! Atishoo! All fall down!" This is a reference to sneezing and disease. It dates from the Middle Ages when the plague swept Europe.

If you caught the disease, an early sign of infection was sneezing. So if you sneezed "atishoo" you were highly likely to fall down and die. Sneezing and coughing were also a way one person passed it on to another. This bout of the plague was called the Black Death. The reason for this was that the poor people suffering the disease often looked an awful slate-blue colour. Other lines in the rhyme, which is really rather a morbid one, are also to do with the illness.

"Ring of Roses" refers to a red rash that was sometimes seen on the skin. "Pocket full of posies" was presumably some flowers to keep away the stench of dead bodies. Of these there were plenty. During the fifteenth century the plague killed a quarter of the population of Europe.

We still have not wiped the disease out. In 1967 over 5,000 cases were seen in South Vietnam.

Incidentally, the disease has the dubious distinction of being the most infectious known. Also, a severe bout is nearly always fatal. No wonder it is still remembered, if only in a nursery rhyme.

"My Dad says you should rest after a big meal."

Neither charging about, as you probably do, nor sleeping in a chair, as your Dad probably does, is ideal. Sleeping in a chair causes a stiff neck. Also when your mouth flops open you breathe through it and it dries out your throat. One reason people sleep sitting up is that a full stomach pushes up on to the chest if you lie flat and this can be uncomfortable.

So what should you do after eating? Some animals do go straight to sleep. This is not surprising. As the *British Medical Journal* has pointed out, it is difficult for the South American boa constrictor to do much else. Imagine trying to wriggle around after you have swallowed a goat, whole!

What about people, though? The first experiment on this was done by a man called the Holy Roman Emperor, Frederick II. He fed two men a big meal each then he rested one for an hour and made the other do exercises. Then he killed them both and had a look inside them. The man who had rested for an hour had digested

his food better than the man who had been running around an arena. (Presumably they didn't know what was going to happen to them as the thought of being killed would almost certainly have affected their digestions.) Some less barbaric tests have been carried out since then and *gentle* exercise is now known to be better than either extreme. That's why a lot of grown-ups like to go for a stroll after Sunday lunch.

I suspect your Dad knows you have never strolled anywhere in your life. In which case resting is best.

The basic reason why digestion suffers if you exercise a lot may be one of blood supply. Digestion of food needs blood. After a meal extra blood is sent to the guts to do this. If you exercise, extra blood is also needed to supply oxygen to the muscles. And if you have a really hot bath, blood is sent to the skin. (You will notice this as a pinkness of the skin and it helps keep your temperature down in the hot bathroom.) However, there is a limited amount of blood to go round. So anything like exercise or a hot bath can make digestion suffer.

This is probably the basis of all the advice you hear about what not to do after a meal.

"My Grandad says he can blow smoke out of his ears. Is this possible?"

A sk him to do it and see. I bet he can't. Unless his eardrum has a big hole in it, there is no direct connection between the mouth and the ear.

"I get car-sick and my Dad says I should open one of the car windows. Does this work?"

It may well do. Car-sickness really bothers some children; but it often goes away when you reach your teens. Most families have a remedy. Some sit on brown paper. Others hang chains from the car. If they work for you, stick with them, even though there is no obvious medical explanation.

Your Dad's method of opening the window probably works by keeping the air fresh and making you look out of the window. If you have something interesting to look at you are less likely to feel ill.

When the first research was done into which pills were best for sea-sickness, soldiers were sent out to sea in rough weather. Some were given a tablet with no drugs in it so that there could be a comparison with the real one. The soldiers did not know this and a lot thought that the dummy tablet was wonderful! Such is the power of suggestion. Pills to prevent car-sickness are now available in various forms. They can be bought at a chemist's and, as one is likely to suit you more than the rest, it's worth trying another if the first has no effect.

At the risk of stating the obvious, remember to take any medicine before you go. It's no use trying to swallow it when you are already being sick.

"My Mum and Dad always make me wash my hands after going to the toilet. Is this a waste of time?"

No. It's *not* a waste of time at all. You will get away with not washing 99 times out of 100, but occasionally germs and worms and other nasties can get passed on to you or to other people from dirty hands.

Just take threadworms as an example. If you wipe your bottom and don't wash your hands any worm eggs that you may have picked up could lodge in your fingernails. Then later they could get back into you if, for example, you put your hands in your mouth. Even worse, other children could catch them if you touched their food or something they would handle or might put in their mouths.

So it's very important to wash your hands after going to the toilet. It is also one reason why you often get told not to bite your nails or put your fingers in your mouth.

Happily worms are easily cleared up by medicine. Still, it is better not to get them in the first place, or give them to anyone else.

"My dentist tells me not to eat sweets. Yet if I go to the doctor I get syrupy medicine. This doesn't make sense."

Doctors have realised that what you say is true and a lot of the liquid medicines are now being made in forms other than sugary syrups.

This is not as easy to do as it sounds.

Sugar is a very useful thing to put in medicine. This is mainly because it can disguise the unpleasant taste which some medicines have. It is also a very good preservative and means that a medicine is less likely to "go off" if it is left on the shelf for a while.

Given the prospect of a patient taking a drug and getting better, even if it means having a small amount of sugar in the mouth for a short time, most doctors will go for the sugary medicines.

Some drugs can be put into a water base instead of a syrup. These medicines can have artificial sweeteners added. However, getting the dose in each measure exact, and – more difficult than that – getting it to stay exact, can be a problem. You do not want the particles of drug in the suspension to settle out. This business of "settling out" is why you have to shake some medicine bottles.

Chemists can find it a big headache making medicine. There are so many things to consider. You may not have realised it but one good reason for using a sticky syrup is that it is more difficult for the patient to spit it out than a watery medicine is!

*"I have been told that eating bread crusts makes
your hair curl."*

This is not true. You are born with a particular type
of hair, according to the pattern of the hair
"follicle" in the scalp. It may be straight, curly or
crinkly; and the colour can vary too. You can change the
shape (with curlers or tongs or perms) and the colour
(with hair dye) but as new hair grows it will go back to
its normal state.

Curly hair often gets straighter as you grow up. This
is because it becomes coarser as you get older and less
inclined to curl.

As a matter of interest, everyone has his or her own
maximum hair length. So left uncut your hair will not
necessarily grow to waist level.

Even standing out in the rain makes no difference,
despite what some people seem to think!

Neither will cutting it. This idea probably comes from
when boys first start to shave. Each time they cut the hair
off on the face it grows back more strongly. The hair *is*
developing. Not because of cutting
it, but because they are growing
into men who need to shave.

Back to the original question.
This is probably just another example
of how adults try to con children into
doing what they don't want to do.

53

"Does chocolate cause problems like spots or migraine?"

First spots. If by "spots" you mean acne, then the strict medical answer is that there is no link. Some young people who suffer with spots cut out chocolate and think it helps. There is no explanation; but it might be worth a try.

Chocolate *can* cause migraine headaches, though. These are more common in children than is generally realised, which is unfortunate since treatment is very helpful. It is important to remember that chocolate isn't always the cause.

If you do have migraines you are in good company. A lot of famous people have had them, like Julius Caesar and George Bernard Shaw. Lewis Caroll is supposed to have dreamed up the idea of *Alice in Wonderland* during the early part of an attack. This early phase of a migraine is in some people an extraordinary experience. As the blood flow changes inside the skull the brain may register all sorts of funny things: hunger, yawning, hallucinations, flashing, exploding lights.

The dazzling light St Paul saw on the road to Damascus could be explained in terms of a migraine. And although Joan of Arc may have had a mental illness, she may have suffered from migraines too.

These symptoms are often not identified as migraines. It tends to be thought of as a condition which only shows itself as a severe one-sided headache. This is why many children with migraine do not get treatment. No one realises what they are describing.

There is some good news, though. About half the children who suffer from migraine grow out of the condition.

"I have heard that fresh air at the seaside is good for you."

It is, actually, for some people, but not for the reasons usually thought. At one time an annual trip to the seaside was for a lot of working people their first breath of unpolluted air all year. Now that our cities and factories have been cleaned up this is not so true. Years ago the air was often described as "bracing" and the magical powers of a gas called ozone were talked about. This was simply clever advertising, trying to get people to visit a particular seaside resort. Ozone is a form of oxygen, but it does not exist in any special beneficial amounts at the seaside. Also it has no special powers. The sea air simply did not irritate the lungs as the air in the coal mines and factories did.

These days there is still one reason why sea air may be healthy, particularly in summer. If you are unlucky enough to have hay fever, the problem of a runny nose, streaming eyes and sometimes wheezing cough are caused by pollen blowing in the wind. Exactly what it is that brings tears to your eyes varies, depending on where you live. In big cities it may be the plane tree. (This was planted all over the place because it does better than other trees in polluted air.) In many country towns the trees causing problems are more likely to be oak and beech. You may be able to guess what is giving you trouble by the time of year. The plane tree is troublesome in May. Symptoms later in the year may be a reaction to dahlias which are pollinated from August to October.

If you go to the seaside and the wind is blowing off the sea there will be no pollen in it as there are no grasses and trees out at sea. So almost instantly hay fever sufferers feel better.

In many ways the best place for someone with hay fever to spend the summer would be on an off-shore oil rig. There the wind comes off the sea from whichever direction it blows. (The rig would have to be a good way out though. These pollens can travel on the wind for seventy to eighty kilometres.)

If you can't organise this, see if your parents will take you to the seaside at weekends in summer!

Another cause of wheezing can be the house dust mite. It was not until the early 1960s that it was realised what allergic problems this little creature was causing. It lives in just about everyone's home. And the place that it likes best is the mattress. Here it finds just the warmth and dampness that suits it. It breeds in late summer; and it is just after this time that the worst symptoms flare up. It's not actually the mite itself that people react to. It's a very clean (eight-legged) beast and when it goes to the toilet (if you can use that expression about a house mite) it wraps everything up in a hard sack. To make this easy to pass, it coats it to make it slide out easily. This coating is what causes the sneezing, runny eyes and asthma. And of course this tends to be worse when you're in bed. Or when you make the bed and bang the mattress.

The house dust mite partly explains why mountain air is said to be clean and fresh. It does not like living up at about 10,000 feet. Before modern treatments children with bad asthma had to be sent to special schools in places like Switzerland. It's now clear that one reason they got better was because the house dust mite does not like cool, dry mountain air.

"Does smoking stunt your growth?"

Smoking really is bad news for lots of reasons. It can make you ill and in this way slow down growth. It's expensive. Money really does go up in smoke. Also it's unpleasant for other people. Smokers smell. If you are unlucky enough to kiss one it's a bit like kissing an ashtray.

Parents want you to grow up "big and strong". So some of them worry about whether or not their children are putting on the right amount of weight for their age. This is understandable because they care for their kids.

Some do go a bit over the top I know. But not the ones who nag about smoking.

Some people joke and call cigarettes coffin nails. Unfortunately there is some truth in the joke. And it's not funny.

"A friend told me if you sneeze with your eyes open they could pop out."

Not true, tell your friend. It's impossible to sneeze with your eyes open. It's just one of those things like speaking while you're breathing in. You can't do it! Try it and see, if you don't believe me.

Your eyes stay in their sockets mainly because of the muscles that attach the two eyes to the bone of the skull.

Each eye has six muscles. They tether the eyeball in its bed of fat within the socket, like a ship with six anchor ropes. The eyelids help a bit as well.

The muscles are what make the eye move so that you can look in different directions without moving your head. (An owl can't do this. It has to move its whole head!)

Two of these eye muscles can pull the eye forward. This in fact is not usually much use. However, it can be a very strong pull.

One negro stage comedian years ago developed this as a trick. He could use the two eye muscles to pull each eye forward and so far out of their sockets that he was able to close his eyelids behind his eyes!

Not something to try. His act finally had to end because his eyes got badly infected.

"When the Queen came on the telly at Christmas my Aunt said she had blue blood. Is this true?"

No. The expression comes from the days generations ago when the rich and privileged did little work outside and so had pale skins. The peasants who toiled all day in the fields went much darker from exposure to the sun and wind.

Veins shine through pale skin and look blue. (You can often see this on the inside of your own wrists where the skin is pale.) So the peasants used to say that their pale rulers had "blue blood" or were blue-blooded.

Incidentally, blood is red because some of its cells

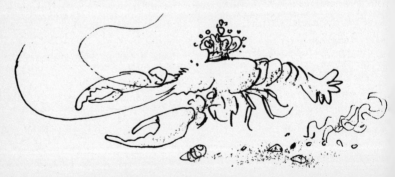

carry haemoglobin. This complex substance contains iron. Its main function is to carry oxygen from the lungs to the rest of the body. The blood is a bright red in the arteries as it is well oxygenated. As the oxygen gets used up the blood goes a much darker colour. This is how it looks on its return journey to the heart and lungs via the veins. Veins tend to be nearer the skin than arteries so they are easier to see.

One group of creatures does not use iron for all this. Shellfish use copper instead. This in fact really is blue. So it is the lobster and its friends that have blue blood, and not the Queen. She has red blood like you and me.

"Is it true that brown eggs are better for you than white eggs?"

No. Inside they are the same. In Britain people seem to prefer brown eggs to white eggs, so the farmers give them brown eggs. In the USA, France and Holland the opposite is true. People get it into their heads that one colour is better than another.

The reasons are not clear. It may be that when eggs of one colour or the other appear to be scarce in the shops, people want the rarer ones and will pay more for them. Farmers then try to provide what the public wants. They do this by finding the right chickens. A general rule is that brown hens produce brown egg shells and white hens white-shelled eggs.

If the farmer wants to change the colour of the yolk and make it darker (some people prefer it this way) he changes the food he gives to the chickens. But food will

not change the colour of the shell. The hen decides that.

Much is made of free-range eggs. These tend to have any colour shell and the yolks are variable because so is the hen's food.

I have a country friend who lets his hens live like this. Most people I know think these free-range eggs are the best.

The hens certainly seem very happy living like this. The eggs are the best I have ever tasted.

It may even be true to say that our world would be a better place if we lived the free and easy life my friend's chickens do.

"My Granny says if you get constipated and don't go to the toilet you get white 'fur' on your tongue."

This is not correct. A lot of the ideas that people have about health stem from things they have seen doctors do. Doctors often look at the tongue when you are unwell because the mouth often gives clues to what is happening elsewhere in the body. However, the common idea about a furry tongue meaning constipation is not one of them. It probably started in the days when people frequently made inaccurate claims for medicines. The people who sold laxatives used to make a lot of fuss about constipation. They must have chosen the sign of having a furred tongue because so many normal people have them. All they were interested in was someone poking his or her tongue out at the mirror, finding some white "fur", and going out to buy their brand of laxative at the chemist.

The two may of course be indirectly linked. Someone ill in bed with a fever may not be eating much, and hence not going to the toilet. They may also have a furred tongue because their nose is blocked and they are breathing through their mouth and tending to dry it out. However, you cannot link the two together directly and say one is causing the other.

The white "fur" is caused by living organisms that occur naturally in everyone's mouth. You can't see them, but if conditions change in the mouth (as when you dry it out a bit by breathing through your mouth) then they multiply and coat the tongue.

There must be hundreds of reasons why the mouth undergoes change. And they can all produce this appearance.

"If I yawn my Mum tells me I'm not getting enough sleep."

She *may* be right. Especially if you are yawning near bedtime. But there could be other explanations.

Yawning is what is called a reflex action. This means it's something that happens automatically without your having to think about it. There are lots of things the body does automatically, which is just as well. Imagine having to remember to breathe all the time. There would not be many people around with poor memories.

The purpose of a yawn is to get more oxygen into the lungs. It's a sort of deep breath. The body has decided you need a boost, perhaps because you are tired.

When you lose interest in something – perhaps a

boring lesson at school – your breathing tends to become less deep and effective. Then comes this clever reflex to put things right.

There is still a lot more to find out about yawning. Why, for example, is the act contagious? I bet some of you have yawned while reading this (and I hope it's not through boredom!).

"My Mum says that she can tell if I am getting enough sleep by looking for bags under my eyes."

She may be able to. It's a lot easier to do it by making a note of when you go to sleep and when you wake up though.

There are a number of reasons that "bags" form under your eyes if you are tired. The first is that it is an area of the body with quite a lot of blood vessels. The skin here is also less elastic. So if blood gathers under the eye, as can happen if you are tired, the area sags into "bags".

Because the skin here is thin extra blood can show through as a dark shadow. When this happens it may look as if there are rings under the eyes.

"If I come in from playing outside, my Mum tells me to take off my coat so that I feel the benefit later when I go back out again."

Y ou could keep your coat on all the time. But it's a waste of the body's own heat-regulating system.

The coat keeps you warm by trapping a layer of warmish air around you in the fibres of the coat. When you come into a heated house this isn't necessary. The body can produce enough heat to keep itself warm. Indeed if the house is hot and your body feels the coat is making you too warm, it will try to lose extra heat.

If you then go out, still with the coat on, the whole process of losing heat has to be slammed into reverse. This is wasteful and you are not feeling the benefit of a heat-saving coat.

It's also worth putting a hat on, as a lot of heat can be lost through the head. Uncovered, it acts like a big, round, wasteful radiator. That's why putting a hat on will help keep your feet warm!

"My uncle lives in the country. He says that you can cure nettle stings by rubbing dock on your skin."

Dock leaves can help a bit. They contain a substance that is not unlike some of the anti-histamine creams that you can buy from the chemist to put on bites and stings. (They are called anti-histamines because histamine is the chemical in the body which is released in response to the nettle sting (or whatever) and causes the itchy rash.) Dock just happens to grow naturally and, rather conveniently, often close to nettles!

What dock contains isn't very powerful, though, and in any case doctors don't think that anti-histamine creams are the best way of dealing with bites and stings. The reason is that although in theory they should help, they often cause more of a problem than they solve. This is because they themselves can cause a reaction.

Going back to nettles and dock leaves, the idea that a remedy will grow near to the source of a problem is a very old one. In medieval times it was called the "doctrine of signatures". It may just be coincidence but it does happen with a number of other plants. For example, fever often occurred in damp marshy places where willow trees grew; and lo and behold they found a drug in willow bark that helped. These days you probably know that drug better as aspirin.

"There is a joke going around at school that eating baked beans makes you fart."

They do. And they really are in a class of their own when it comes to this.

People who eat a high fibre diet "let off" a lot because the fibre is not digested and gets broken down in the bowel to give off gas. (I have a friend who calls this "fluffing"!) Peas and sprouts are famous for this too. (If you do change to a high fibre diet this problem usually settles down after a few weeks.)

Baked beans appear to have two complex sugars in them that produce the wind. The extra gas is in fact hydrogen, which tends not to smell. So wind from beans is not so anti-social. Scientists have been trying to make a wind-free bean, so far with little success.

In case you're wondering who has the job of collecting this wind and studying it for hydrogen, it's actually done by measuring the hydrogen in the breath, using something like the police's breathalyser. Just as breath alcohol tells you what the blood alcohol level is, breath hydrogen tells you how much hydrogen is in the gut. There is no need to wait for it to come out.

Methane is another gas made inside the bowel. (A similar thing happens at the bottom of a stagnant pond when leaves rot to form smelly gases.) But not all wind in the gut comes from food breakdown. Some has been swallowed with food. Nervous people tend to gulp down a lot like this.

The average person passes about 0.5 litres of gas per day. That's the volume of a milk bottle. This is not done all at once. Again, taking an average person – say like my friend – she can expect to "fluff" 13 times a day!

The smell varies a great deal as I expect you have

found out. The classic "rotten egg" smell comes from the gas hydrogen sulphide. This is produced if you eat a lot of meat because of the sulphur it contains. Meat is made of what are called amino acids. Two of these in meat contain sulphur (chemical symbol S). Hydrogen sulphide's chemical formula is H_2S. A lot of meat means a lot of "S" and hence a lot of smelly H_2S.

Beans making only extra hydrogen (H) are thus not so bad. Hydrogen on its own does not smell.

Not all the hydrogen is in the air in the bowel. This lightest of the chemical elements occurs throughout the tissues of the body. In fact it has been worked out that

there is enough in a person to fill a balloon that would take you up into the sky.

There are all sorts of things in my friend's "fluffs". This could be a fairly typical one:

FART
Nitrogen   60 per cent ⎱ This main fraction
Hydrogen   20 per cent ⎰ does not smell
The rest is a mixture of carbon dioxide, methane, oxygen and hydrogen sulphide

AIR
Nitrogen   79 per cent
Oxygen   20 per cent
then traces of carbon dioxide, water and "noble" gases like Argon

A "noble" substance is one which will rarely combine with another. (Like the "H" and "S" uniting to form the rotten egg smell of H_2S.)

There's probably even a little of this nobility in farts as they contain swallowed air.

"Some people say you should put a steak on a black eye."

This is a complete waste of time and good meat. There isn't much you can do once the damage is done. Neither is much ever necessary. An ice pack is sometimes used to try to reduce the swelling. This may be important in a game like rugby because if the eye closes the player may have to leave the field.

A black eye is a bruise around the eye and it will come out in the way that any other bruise has to.

When you hurt yourself blood leaks out of damaged blood vessels into the surrounding tissue. It goes dark blue-black because its pigment, haemoglobin, loses its oxygen as it lies in the tissue. Usually this is just under the skin so you can see it.

Days later the bruise turns to green and yellow. This is because of further changes in the pigment.

The "green" colour is the same green as in green bile. What is happening is basically what happens routinely every day as the liver makes bile.

Bile does a lot of things. Just one job is to get rid of old red blood cells. Every red cell in your body lasts about four months. This continual turnover means over 2 million have to be made every second by a grown-up. (It's about half this number in children.) The other side of the coin is that there is a lot of unwanted material for the body to throw out. Unlike household rubbish which gets taken away perhaps once a week when the refuse collector calls, waste from old red blood cells is going out all the time.

Much is saved of course. The body is clever enough to save old blood protein. Also iron is taken and stored. But the pigments are not needed. These go out via the liver's ducts into the alimentary tract. From there it's a journey of some 8.5 metres until they finally leave the body. (By this time they are a brown colour as you may have noticed.) Their original green-yellow colour (the same colour you see in an old bruise) is what gives the bile its well known appearance.

So what you see in a bruise as it changes colour and fades is the everyday process involved in the normal turnover of red blood cells.

"My parents say you should have a good hot breakfast before going to school."

The first thing that I can say for certain is that it needn't be hot. There's little extra benefit from having hot food. Food soon heats up when it gets inside you. It is after digestion that the real "heat" of the food is released.

Now to the question of whether it matters if you go to school without breakfast. If you really don't want anything to eat and, more important, are not going off to school and filling up later with junk food, then it may be that for some reason your body doesn't need food in the morning. It is unusual, though, not to want *anything*. There was some famous research done in America over forty years ago which showed that if children did not have breakfast in the morning they did not do so well either physically or mentally later in the day. Not everyone agrees with this research. And it has been repeated without this conclusion being confirmed.

One well-known doctor who specialised in looking after children has compared this meal to filling up a car with petrol. Your Dad does not need to do this every morning before he drives to work. The car will work perfectly well half-full. This is important common-sense advice, for one thing is sure: a battle over food is one which nobody wins. You are just likely to get indigestion.

The final point is that you do need to eat good food some time during the day in order to grow. Make sure that if you miss breakfast, you get the necessary nourishment at some other time in the day. If you don't, you will be the one who suffers in the end.

"I like crisps and cheesy things, but grown-ups expect me to like sweet things."

Some adults do expect children to like sweets. It has been traditional for years to give sweets as a present or a reward for "being good". Also at meal-times the "sweet" course is often thought of as the frivolous, enjoyable thing to finish off with, after you have eaten what is "good for you". People have become conditioned to this pattern of eating. It doesn't always occur to grown-ups that you might prefer to finish a meal with cheese and biscuits instead.

One reason for liking or disliking different flavours

lies on the tongue. It recognises four basic flavours with its taste buds: bitter, sweet, sour and salt. When you are young you have more sweet buds than when you grow up, so a sweet food will set more nerve ends tingling now than later in life.

Another reason could be that when you are young you need a lot of energy for growing and charging about. Sugar provides this.

By the way, the sweet taste buds tend to be on the tip of the tongue. Just the part you lick a lolly with! The bitter ones are towards the back. If you watch grown-ups gulping bitter beer back this could be why. The real taste comes when the bitter hits the back of the tongue. That's one reason, anyway . . .

"Why is our teacher always telling us not to share things like combs, towels and shoes?"

Lots of reasons. The main one is to prevent the spread of various infections. These could be nits (comb), pink eye or conjunctivitis (towels), or athlete's foot (shoes). There could be other reasons though. If you wear someone else's shoes and they don't fit, you could hurt your feet. You could also catch a verruca. A verruca is a wart that has been flattened into the foot by the weight of the body. They are caused by a virus and spread easily. That's why you may be asked to wear some form of foot covering if you go swimming.

It's worth saying a word about feet here. I can remember being told that wearing plimsolls or any shoe with a flat heel could make you flat-footed. This is nonsense. Until the age of four we all had flat feet anyway. The arch was simply filled with fat. This is normal.

You can do a test by standing on tiptoe. It will be obvious if there is an arch or if the bottom of the foot really is flat.

Feet vary in shape and flat feet are not really the dreadful problem a lot of grown-ups think they are. If your feet really *are* flat, the exercise to do is to pick up marbles with your toes!

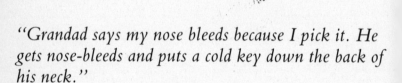

"Grandad says my nose bleeds because I pick it. He gets nose-bleeds and puts a cold key down the back of his neck."

He is right about the nose-picking. Nine times out of ten the blood comes from an area just inside the nose on the partition between the two nostrils. It is easily reached by a finger and bleeds easily if the veins are damaged. It's called Little's area after a New York surgeon called James Little who died in 1885.

Your Grandad is wrong about using a key. This popular remedy is worse than useless. Not only does it not stop nose-bleeds, but if you tilt your head back the blood runs down your throat and can make you choke.

The best way to stop it is to pinch the nose firmly below the bridge and lean forward with your mouth open over a bowl. (You need to let the blood drip out of your mouth.) Breathe through the mouth for at least ten minutes and the bleeding will nearly always stop. It is very important not to blow your nose or sniff for a while, otherwise the bleeding will start again. A clot must be allowed to form. The time you have to pinch the nose is related to the time it takes to stop a bleed. Bleeding stops in two basic ways. These are measured as the clotting time and the bleeding time.

Blood taken and put in a bottle will form a lumpy clot in about ten minutes. This is the clotting time. It depends on clotting factors in the blood itself. The other way is measured by the bleeding time, which is the time it takes to stop bleeding from a wound like a pin prick. This is about two to six minutes. Bleeding stops because small blood vessels clamp down to stop the leak. The two factors usually help each other out when you cut yourself. (So if anyone asks you what a clot is, you now know. Also you can tell them what the bleeding time is!)

There are a lot of things which can influence this process. Some people with a disease called haemophilia have a clotting factor missing (number 8 to be precise). Their clotting time is long. If they cut themselves they can bleed for weeks. This condition is passed on in families and it is the boys who suffer the bleeding. The girls simply carry the problem on to the next generation.

Some of the Royal families of Europe have been affected with haemophilia in the past. This seems to have started with Queen Victoria. She passed it on to, among others, the Russian Royal family. Her great-grandson Alexis was one of them. One of the ways that the "mad monk" Rasputin impressed himself on the Russian Royal family was by trying to treat the bouts of bleeding

Alexis suffered from. A common problem that haemo-philiacs have is that they bleed into their own joints, such as the knees. This is incredibly painful. Rasputin was able to help Alexis, and thus impress the boy's mother, the Tsarina, because he was able to get Alexis to relax. This form of suggested relaxation is no more than hypnotism. Rasputin used it as a very powerful tool in a lot of things he did. In treating the boy, though, it worked because a lot of the pain in this sort of illness is the result of muscle spasm. Get the muscles to relax and a lot of the pain goes. Rasputin was hailed as a medical magician. These days doctors who are good at this sort of thing are often said to have a good bedside manner. Rasputin's bedside manner was apparently brilliant.

So many things affect blood clotting. Another inter-esting one is a substance called adrenalin. It makes blood more sticky. It's produced in the body by a gland that sits on top of the kidneys, and it tends to pour out into the blood when you are frightened or anxious. It's what makes your heart beat faster when you are being told off.

Adrenalin gets a body ready for action in many ways. Breathing speeds up. Muscles get more blood (diverted from the skin, so you go pale). Sugar is produced for energy. The eyes widen. And there are even some unfortunate effects. The guts work overtime and so food shoots through quickly. So fright can really make you run in more ways than one.

Adrenalin's effect in making the blood sticky may account for something some people notice when they go to the dentist to have a tooth out. Things are all right in the dentist's chair. But when you get home the tooth socket suddenly starts bleeding. This may be because the fear of the dentist was helping to stop any bleeding. When you get home and relax and the adrenalin wears off, the blood is less sticky. So it bleeds out of the hole where the tooth was.

"My Grandad says he used to have to brush his hair a hundred times a day."

This was presumably to avoid getting head lice. Their eggs are called nits and look like tiny grains of rice. Lice don't like being hit by a comb or brush as it bashes them about and they can't get settled around the base of a hair. It may literally knock their legs off. Once they do get anchored and start laying eggs you can have a problem.

So no legs means no eggs.

There are some good treatments nowadays, but in the same way as your Grandad had to, it is better to keep them at bay by brushing or combing. Also it makes your hair look neater.

"I have been told that if you frown and the wind changes your face will stay that way."

This is obviously not true. To smile uses about seventeen muscles and to frown just over forty, so perhaps this old wives' tale is trying to tell us all something.

"Do carrots make you see in the dark? Or, put another way, have you ever seen a rabbit with glasses?"

In a way, yes, carrots do help you see in the dark. The orange colour of carrots, carotene, helps make Vitamin A in the body. Vitamin A is necessary if you are going to see in the dark. It helps special nerves in the eye work. These are called rods. Chickens have no rods and in fact are blind at night!

Lots of vegetables have this carotene. The special link between carrots and seeing in the dark was made in the Second World War. The RAF's fighter pilots needed good vision to fly at night, to reduce the chance of being shot down. In an attempt to try anything they were told to eat lots of carrots. It did no harm; but probably did no good. But the idea that carrots could give you night vision spread. People were encouraged to "Dig for Victory" and to grow their own vegetables and soon everyone started saying carrots made you see in the dark.

A twist to the story is that the device Radar was being developed. This really did give the pilots "extra" vision. It was important to keep Radar secret from the enemy for as long as possible. So it was very convenient if carrots were given the credit instead. These untruths called propaganda are commonly put about during wars.

It is important not to think that *extra* Vitamin A will do you good. In fact it may poison you. Also there have been silly people who have eaten so many carrots that their skin has gone yellow. Everything in moderation.

Eskimos and husky dogs will not eat polar bear liver. Somehow they know it contains so much Vitamin A that it will make them ill. The early explorers had no such instinct. In 1912 two hungry men on an Australasian

Antarctic expedition ate the liver of their husky-dog. One died and the other was very ill. Large areas of their skin just peeled off. Nearly fifty years passed before the truth was realised. Just 113 grams of husky-dog liver contains a poisonous dose of Vitamin A.

"When there was an eclipse of the sun we were made to look at it through dark glasses."

This can be very tricky. If you look directly at a very bright light like the sun you could go permanently blind. The back of the eye would be literally sunburnt.

You may have done a similar thing using a magnifying lens and a piece of paper. Focus the sun on to the paper and you can burn a hole in it. Do not do this with your eyes!

It is best never to look directly at the sun. As a boy I was taught you could look at the sun (I wanted to watch an eclipse) through smoked glass. The trouble is that if it's not sufficiently "smoked" then enough sunlight will get through to do the damage. It's the same with dark glasses. The risk of going blind is too great to take chances. Even clever people have made this mistake. Galileo looked at the sun when he was pefecting the first telescope and he went partially blind as a result.

So if you want to look at the sun do it indirectly. One way is to use a mirror to reflect the sun's light on to a piece of paper. (Note that the paper will not burn. This is because there is no lens to focus the rays on to one point.)

A more common problem with bright light is dazzle.

This can be dangerous if you are riding your bike in the dark. What happens is that the sudden glare of a car's headlights shines on to the back of the eye and bleaches out a substance called visual purple.

The result is just like a photographic film being exposed. It takes time for more visual purple to be made so just for a while you may not be able to see. This can be dangerous in traffic.

Visual purple is very interesting. When you go into a dark room it takes about 30 minutes to become fully accustomed to the gloom. This is because visual purple has been bleached out by normal light levels and has to be replaced. After this has happened the eyes are a thousand times more sensitive to light than during the day.

One thing about visual purple is that it really only works with green and blue light. So these colours tend to show up better at dusk. You may have noticed how well green grass shows up in moonlight.

The other side of the coin is that a red light hardly affects it at all. So during the war night-fighter pilots wore red goggles before they flew. This protected visual purple from being bleached out and when the pilots took off the goggles to fly there was no waiting for full night vision.

It works the other way round. Going from dark to very bright light can be very uncomfortable. When batsmen walk out to the crease from a darkened pavilion they have to let their eyes get used to the glare of the sunlight. A similarly uncomfortable feeling can occur when your bedroom light is switched on in the morning.

"My granny says that green apples will make me run to the toilet."

One green apple is unlikely to. However, fruits do contain various sugars, such as glucose, fructose and sucrose. Both green and ripe apples (and pears incidentally) contain a lot of this one called fructose. If too much of this gets loaded too quickly into the first part of the bowel it can't cope. So the partly digested food is moved quickly on to the second part. This can cause belly ache and make you run to the toilet.

Another reason is that apples are high in fibre. This also speeds up the passage of the apple through you.

It is only recently that the limitations of the bowel in dealing with fructose have been realised. It has been known for a long time, though, what fruit can do to your insides. In the days before apples were imported they would suddenly become available at one time of the year when the home-grown crop was picked. Some greedy people ate too many too soon. Then they suffered for it.

A word about the famous prune would not be out of place at this point! In addition to the way that apples work on the bowel, prunes actually contain something extra, a substance that acts to make the muscle in the bowel more active. That is why prunes are sometimes recommended to help you go to the toilet.

There is even a world record for prune eating. Perhaps it should be sponsored by the people who make toilet paper!

"I have trouble getting to sleep when I stay at my friend's house. Grandad says he can sleep better if he sleeps North to South."

It's a matter of doing whatever does the trick for you. If your Grandad finds he can sleep better a certain way then it obviously does work *for him*. Charles Dickens also found this method effective. However, there is no magic in it. There is no evidence that it is due to the earth's magnetic field.

You probably do not sleep at your friend's house for a number of reasons. There are new things to think about. You may not be perfectly relaxed. The general noise level in the evening may be different from that in your bedroom at home. You may be sharing with your friend whereas you usually sleep alone. There are so many reasons why people do not sleep for a night or two.

Good luck if you find a novel way to get off to sleep. Doctors may not be able to explain them, but they are often a lot safer than pills.

So it's a case of whatever turns you off.

"My Mum tells me to run the tap in the morning before having a drink of water."

This is because she is worried about lead getting into your body. At one time the water pipes in houses were made of this heavy metal. Small amounts could dissolve in the water, then slowly, over a long time, build up in the body. This harmed some children.

Things have changed now because plastic and copper pipes are used. However, there are still some old houses with lead pipes.

When the Water Board tests for lead, as it does from time to time to be careful, it tests the water that comes out of the tap first thing in the morning. This is because the water has been undisturbed in the pipe all night and if lead is there it will be relatively concentrated and easier to measure.

87

Perhaps this is where your Mum's idea came from.

There are a number of these heavy metals which are poisonous. They include mercury, thallium, cadmium, antimony and the infamous arsenic. They all tend to cause similar symptoms, although how they get into the body varies quite a lot.

Arsenic is probably the best known heavy metal poison. It was a favourite among murderers as you could buy it easily without arousing suspicion. (It's contained in some weedkillers and even used to be in certain medicines.) Given in small amounts it will slowly kill a person and the symptoms of weight loss, headache and feeling sick and tired are common to many illnesses. Unless there was a reason to be suspicious, a doctor seeing a patient with these problems would think of a lot of other diseases before arsenic poisoning.

Because one dose takes between 10 and 70 days to pass out of the body, amounts given little and often by a poisoner will build up and slowly kill the victim fairly easily.

One thing which arsenic does is to become stored in hair and nails. So it is possible if suspicions are aroused later to find it and prove that the poison was the real cause of death. Often bodies were dug up after burial for this – perhaps when the poisoner was caught poisoning someone else.

"Is it true that you should drink water from the cold tap rather than the hot one?"

Y es, according to my local Water Board. Cold water that comes directly from the main supply has not been stored in any sort of tank in the house. Exactly how you are connected up to the water supply depends on the individual house or flat or bungalow. A lot of houses have what's called a header tank in the loft. This can become contaminated. I have a friend who left her tank uncovered, then later found a mouse had fallen into it.

One thing worth saying is that the hot water from the tap is hardly ever the same hot water that runs through any radiator system that you may have.

Ask your Mum or Dad how your house is connected up to the water. It varies a lot and is interesting. My tank is well covered and the hot water is quite safe to drink.

"Why does Granny always go on about giving me onions when I have a cold?"

B ecause onions give off vapours which make your airways run with fluid. You notice this when you peel one. The extra secretion may make your nose run. It may make more fluid in the lung. This sounds an odd way of treating a cold, but in fact it makes phlegm on the chest easier to cough up as it is less sticky. Many of these old remedies have good reasons behind them. They tend

to date from before antibiotics became available in the 1940s. Then they were all the help there was.

Some old remedies are nonsense of course. One "cure" for whooping cough involved eating a fried mouse. (Some older patients of mine who were given this as children tell me it tastes similar to fried chicken.)

It is easy to laugh at these beliefs until you remember how common whooping cough used to be and what a terrible disease it is.

"Should you feed a cold and starve a fever?"

This is a pretty good general rule. It was certainly a very useful working guide in the old days before doctors and medicines were readily available to everyone.

About "feed a cold" first. Before you start school you are quite likely to have six to twelve "colds" a year. After this it falls off a bit, but in winter colds are very common and nearly all healthy kids can expect quite a few. So can grown-ups who mix with them. Now if you were starved every time you caught a cold it follows that you would spend a fair amount of the winter hungry. It would also affect your growth.

So the "old wives" knew that if you had a cold – an illness which does not produce a fever – you could and should eat. Perhaps that was all there was to it.

Now "starve a fever". This isn't such a simple one.

In quite a lot of very different and sometimes serious conditions the patient has a high temperature. Along with this may come a poor appetite. The "old wives" realised this and knew that the patient either would not or could not stomach food. It was common sense not to force food into someone when it would only make them more sick.

This may sound obvious now, but the saying comes from the days when all the advice a sick child could get in the middle of the night came from a wise "old wife" who was not medically trained. A lot of poor folk years ago had to rely on good advice like this because there were no doctors available to help them.

There may be a scientific explanation too. There is a region in Africa called the Sahel. People who live there often have times of famine. One interesting result of this is that when they are "starving" they are much better at resisting the infectious feverish disease malaria. When they get food again one problem seems to be that they have more trouble with the malaria.

One theory is that if the body goes without food the germs suffer more than the body. So in starving a fever you are making life tough for the germs. The body may do this automatically. When your temperature goes up you lose interest in food.

"An older boy at school says that talking to yourself is the first sign of madness."

This is just the sort of stupid thing that worries normal people and is unkind to those who are really mentally ill.

Most children talk out loud when they are playing on their own. It is all part of make-believe to talk to your toy soldiers or dolls or whatever. Grown-ups sometimes talk to themselves when they are trying to concentrate on something, or to decide what to do next.

There is an indirect basis for this saying. There is one form of mental illness, called schizophrenia, in which the sufferer hears voices. They are very real to that patient, and he or she may reply out loud to the "voices". This may seem very strange to other people nearby who cannot hear anything. It may be that Joan of Arc (who I suggested might have had migraine) had this illness too. As is well known, she heard voices which told her to fight for France.

Another thing which is often said is that hairs on the palm of the hand are a sign of madness. (Then the joker usually says that the second sign is looking for them.) This too may be based partly on fact. There is a rare condition called porphyria in which certain body chemicals go wrong. In one variety of this the sufferer is born with such a problem that the skin burns in sunlight, hair grows on the face and hands, and the teeth become reddish in colour. Because of the effects of the sunlight the person may become hideously scarred, and only feel able to go out in the dark. Years ago these unhappy people roaming the forests at night with scarred faces, red teeth and covered with hair may have been the origins of the legends about werewolves. Porphyria may have started the story about hair on the hands, too.

As a matter of interest, there is yet another form of porphyria with historical connections. An English king, George III, may have had it, and it could have been why he went mad. He certainly went through all sorts of terrible treatments and humiliations because no one understood what was happening to him. Nowadays no one would ever treat this condition by strapping the patient in a chair and slapping on burning poultices.

It is likely that a lot of mental illness will one day turn out to have a cause that everyone can understand, just as has happened with this condition porphyria. Perhaps the mentally ill will then get the sympathy they deserve.

"Do poisonous mushrooms only grow under trees?"

N o. It is very important not to eat anything growing out of doors unless you are sure what it is. Identifying mushrooms, toadstools and wild berries can be difficult, even for experts, so do not eat anything until you have *really* checked it out.

The idea that poisonous mushrooms only grew under trees probably started because one of the best known and most dangerous mushrooms *does* usually grow under trees in light woodland. Under oak and beech to be exact. This is the feared death cap mushroom. It is a killer. It looks a bit like the edible mushroom, except it has white gills underneath. (The edible mushrooms are brown.) The problem is that at the button stage you cannot see the gills. So be very careful of so-called "button" mushrooms growing wild.

It is true that the death cap tends not to grow out in the open and the edible one, like the field and horse mushroom, do; but the price is so high if you make a mistake that you must never, never eat anything until your parents are sure it's all right. This goes for berries, bulbs and everything else in the garden, parks or countryside.

It's worth learning about this for another reason. There are some very tasty mushrooms that do grow under trees. The prince of mushrooms as far as taste goes is the *Agaricus augustus* and this grows in pine forests.

Some plants can hurt you just by touching them. Everyone knows the stinging-nettle. Its leaves have needle-like hairs which break off when you touch them and irritate the skin. Some people say that if you grasp the nettle firmly it will not do this. It's a nice saying. I must say I would prefer someone else to show me that it worked rather than try it myself.

Another plant you should not touch is the giant hogweed. This tall plant grows to over 450 cm. It is a big ow parsley. When it is at its peak in July, be very careful f it. It can produce nasty, burn-like blisters. These are specially painful if you have cut the plant down and put ne hollow stem to your lips as some sort of trumpet or lowpipe.

Finally I'll mention another poisonous plant, the eadly nightshade, which has purple flowers. Its Latin ame is *Atropa belladonna*. (*Bella donna* means "beautiful ady" in Italian.) One of the poisons it contains is the ubstance atropine. One effect of atropine is to widen the upils of the eyes. The plant is called *belladonna* because t one time atropine was used by women to widen their upils. They thought it made them more attractive to nen. (Research has shown this to be true. Some men vere given two nearly identical pictures of a lady. One in act had wider pupils than the other. The men seemed to refer this one although they did not realise why.) Whether it worked or not, however, can hardly have nattered much since using atropine in this way blurs ne vision. The women could not see their boyfriends learly anyway!

So back to the woods. Play safe and don't eat anything rowing wild. But if you do, and you're in doubt, spit it ut.

*"When we went on holiday we had to get up at
5 o'clock in the morning to catch the plane home.
My brother Edward said we should each bang our
heads on the pillow five times to make sure we woke
up."*

I have often had to get up very early for a breakfast
TV show and, though I usually wake up just before I
have to, an alarm call is much more reliable.

Perhaps concentrating on an important time like this
means you sleep less deeply. No one fully understands
the brain's built-in clock. No one really understands the
brain full stop. Even though three-quarters of it is water
it's still better than any computer that's been built!

Try some of this pillow-banging tonight and see if it
works for *you*. There are so many things like this in life
that you can only find out for yourself.